SUMMARY & REVIEW

Heather McGhee

THE SUM

OF US

WHAT RACISM COSTS EVERYONE AND HOW WE CAN PROSPER TOGETHER

DR. JACKSON CARTER ANDERSON

MW00928021

Copyright©2022 Dr. Jackson Carter Anderson

All Rights Reserved

Contents

INTRODUCTION

The summary and analysis in this book are meant as an introduction or companion to your reading experience by providing the key insights and overall essence of a formidable work. This book is not intended as a substitute for the work that it summarizes and analyzes and it is not authorized, approved, licensed or endorsed by the work's author or publisher.

CHAPTER ONE

What is the benefit to me? Learn about the true cost of white supremacy and how to combat it.

White supremacy took center stage when far-right organizations seized the US Capitol in November 2020. The Proud Boys, for example, walked around with Confederate flags, becoming the face of bigotry in the United States.

However, racism existed before the Proud Boys and the Trump presidency. It is intimately intertwined into the history of the United States, dating back to the country's creation by European colonists who established racial hierarchies in order to legitimize slavery and generations of racial discrimination.

In these blinks, you'll understand how America's racial heritage pervades every facet of politics and public life today. You'll learn how politicians purposefully incite racist anger in order to persuade white people to vote against their own economic interests. Most importantly, you'll discover how to advocate for change. We can all profit from the solidarity dividend if we address white supremacy and injustice directly.

You'll find out in a flash.

•Why public pools in the United States were filled with dirt in the 1950s;

•How Somali refugees rescued a struggling Maine manufacturing town; and

•Discuss the relationship between racism and climate change.

CHAPTER TWO

White Americans have been led astray by the zero-sum mindset.

Consider a bucket full of crabs desperately attempting to flee to freedom. The crabs could readily scale the bucket's walls if they climbed on each other's backs. Instead, they continue to pull each other down in a swirl of flailing pincers, going nowhere.

Many people in today's America are in the same predicament as those crabs. Most Americans are stressed as a result of economic uncertainty, decaying public infrastructure, and environmental concerns. And yet, in the last election cycle, the vast majority of white Americans opted for an unashamed pro-rich, climate-change denial, who has proved that he will only exacerbate these issues. Why would white people operate in this manner against their own interests? Because they believe that advancements for Black people come at the expense of their own.

The main point here is that white Americans have been duped into thinking in a zero-sum paradigm.

Maureen Craig and Jennifer Richeson, psychologists, investigated how racial resentment influences white people's political opinions. They showed respondents newspaper articles about how racial minorities might become the majority by 2042 as part of a study. People who regarded changing demographics as a threat to their own position were far more likely to have conservative views on contentious political topics such as raising the minimum wage or outlawing fossil fuels.

Conservative politicians have long grasped this psychology. They are experts at instilling racial concerns and anger among their voters. For example, benefit assistance is presented as a handout to Black people who are too lazy to work. Green energy bills are presented as a rejection of white miners.

Fears that white people are being targeted make no logic. White households had 13 times the wealth of Black households on average. Whites outweigh Blacks in homeownership and are considerably overrepresented in government and high-level positions. So, why are they so concerned about losing?

To truly comprehend the zero-sum paradigm, one must go back to the formation of the United States, to the European colonists who enslaved Africans and took indigenous land in order to establish a new country. They required a moral justification for their actions. As a result, they created a racial hierarchy in which Black people were at the bottom. Because of this system, they were able to legitimize slavery, which funded the establishment of modern America. White people literally made their fortunes off of Black suffering. White people are terrified of equality because they fear that the zero-sum paradigm will be flipped, and they will be the losers this time. Nothing could be further from the truth, as you'll witness in the next blink.

CHAPTER THREE

Racism has long harmed public services.

Consider the following scenario: a gleaming public swimming pool, once the pride of Montgomery, Alabama, has been filled with filth, rendering it inoperable. What's the reason? A court declared in 1959 that the pool had to be desegregated and that it had to be open to all members of the public, including Black people, as a public commodity.

Civil rights organizations around the country were scoring huge victories in court cases challenging the constitutionality of segregated public services. Instead of allowing for integrated public pools, administrators sought to completely dismantle the public pool infrastructure. Some pools were leased to private clubs with whites-only membership requirements. Others were permitted to decay slowly due to a lack of investment. Others, such as the Montgomery pool, were completely closed down. White folks stopped supporting public services when the "public" included Black people.

The main point here is that racism has consistently degraded public services.

Following the Great Depression, President Franklin D. Roosevelt instituted the New Deal in 1933. The government underwrote cheap mortgages, reinforced job security, and provided comprehensive social programs to the underprivileged under this initiative. Until the 1950s, these governmental programs were supported by 70% of the white population.

But there was a catch: Black people were virtually always excluded, whether through clear legislative provisions or covert methods like redlining. This refers to maps made in the 1930s to determine which locations banks judged dangerous. Areas with a high concentration of Black population were often labeled as dangerous. Most Black homebuyers were thus ineligible for state-subsidized New Deal mortgages.

The New Deal measures helped to develop a strong white middle class. But all changed when Black people pushed for a piece of the pie during the civil rights protests of the

1960s. White support for an activist government has decreased to roughly 35%, where it currently stands.

Why would white people suddenly turn against government initiatives that had long benefited them? Because they were afraid of what would happen if Black people had equal access to opportunities. White economic superiority has existed for so long that it has become entirely invisible. White prosperity appears to be the product of a stronger work ethic or "bootstraps mindset," rather than generous – and discriminating – state initiatives such as the New Deal.

If Black people could benefit from the same public services as white people, the economic hierarchy, and so the artificial racial hierarchy, could be upended. Instead of swimming together, white folks drained the pools, harming everyone.

CHAPTER FOUR

Racism undermines democracy in the United States.

Many pundits condemned the unprecedented attacks on US democracy when armed protestors laid siege to the US Capitol to protest the results of the 2020 elections.

These attacks, however, are not new. At its core, democracy is the notion that all citizens can have a say in how their country is managed through voting in elections. However, this ideal has always been jeopardized. For a long time, Black people in the United States were not considered citizens. Today, racist voter suppression laws undermine democracy by preventing hundreds of thousands of people from voting.

The main point is that racism is harmful to democracy in the United States.

The US constitution was structured from the beginning to give wealthy white men the maximum power. Only white male landowners were allowed to vote in the first elections. Even after the Fifteenth Amendment made racial discrimination unlawful, governments devised inventive tactics to suppress Black voters. Mississippi, for example, implemented poll fees - a two-dollar levy for voting, almost equivalent to 57 dollars today. They also imposed additional restrictions, such as literacy tests and inspections of "good character," before residents could vote.

This effectively excluded the vast majority of the Black population. However, it also excluded a large number of poor white individuals who lacked the wherewithal to pay the poll taxes. Many Southern states used voting suppression measures, which effectively killed democracy. By 1944, poll tax states had only 18 percent voter participation, compared to 69 percent nationally.

Unfortunately, voter suppression measures like this are not a historical curiosity. They still exist in some form now. For example, all voters must be registered, yet voter registration regulations vary from state to state. In Republican states such as Texas, lawmakers have mandated that voters show certain photo identification, declaring that gun permits are acceptable but college IDs are not. Given that gun owners are overwhelmingly white, these rules are clearly discriminatory and designed to create bureaucratic barriers for Black voters. Other states, such as Ohio, have begun to deregister voters who did not vote in past elections.

Voter suppression laws were designed with Black voters in mind, but conservative politicians' efforts have expanded to include young white voters as well. What else could explain North Carolina's decision to discontinue a program that automatically registers high school students? Or moved polling places so they weren't near college campuses?

Voter suppression jeopardizes the fundamental foundation of democracy: the notion that everyone has a seat at the table.

CHAPTER FIVE

Racial animosity hurts unions and puts workers against one another.

Workers at the Nissan automobile manufacturing factory in Canton, Mississippi, were given the opportunity to vote on whether or not to join a union in 2017.

The potential rewards were enormous: joining a union meant they could fight for greater healthcare and retirement benefits, higher salaries, and a safer workplace collectively.

Despite all of these benefits, white workers voted against forming a union by a margin of 500 votes. Why would these workers vote against themselves? Because they'd fell for an old ruse. They'd been made to believe that Black employees' opportunities would come at the expense of their own.

The main point here is that racial resentment undermines unions and pits workers against one another.

These concerns were not entirely unwarranted. In fact, Nissan factory managers made certain that white workers who followed the rules received preferential treatment. While black laborers sweated on the perilous assembly line, white workers did the cushier, safer occupations, such as examining automobiles before they left the factory floor. Fighting for equality would level the playing field. However, it would significantly enhance working conditions and pay for everyone. So, why were white workers ready to forego the opportunity for fundamentally improved working circumstances in return for a few perks?

Unions were not always so racially divided. Indeed, multiracial union organization was responsible for the tremendous victories we now take for granted, such as the 40-hour workweek and retirement benefits. In the 1950s, one out of every three American workers joined to a labor organization. However, in the early 1960s, this figure began to fall, and unions began to lose bargaining leverage. This happened to coincide with civil rights protests in the 1960s, which were supported by some of the most prominent unions. Politicians and business lobbyists began to use race politics to build discontent in unions, portraying them as protecting lazy Black workers who don't want to work hard. Only one out of every sixteen American workers is a member of a union today.

While the Canton experience may make us skeptical of the chances for cross-racial organizing, another workers' movement provides optimism. Fast food workers from all over New York began protesting for greater wages in 2012, dubbed the "Fight for 15." This movement prioritizes racial harmony in its campaigns. The results have been extremely effective, with cities around the country voting to raise the minimum wage to $15 per hour. Working together truly pays off.

CHAPTER SIX

Climate change cannot be addressed without addressing racism.

We've all seen images of hurricanes storming down US coastlines, wildfires ravaging forests, and malnourished polar bears perched on melting ice caps. Climate change is portrayed as having a single main adversary: greedy companies that bribe politicians to maintain the massive fossil fuel industries. We don't typically associate racism with political inaction on climate change. However, we are overlooking one essential aspect of the situation.

The main point here is that you can't tackle climate change without also fighting racism.

It's no coincidence that white opposition to climate change policies grew after Obama was elected president. Conservative lawmakers portrayed Obama as prepared to sacrifice white employment, such as mining, to advance his environmental goals. It became a zero-sum game once more. With racist overtones, the environment vs the economic.

Indeed, race is an important indication of whether or not you are willing to battle global warming. According to polls, less than 25% of white individuals polled are concerned about climate change, compared to 70% of Black people. White people who voiced racial hatred were far more inclined to deny climate change.

The political and corporate elites who oppose climate change action are almost always rich white men. Even if they believe in the significance of global warming, their zero-sum mentality leads them to assume they can shield themselves from the consequences. To some extent, this is correct. Landfills and incinerators are nearly always located in Black areas, dubbed "sacrifice zones." As a result, the health repercussions of pollution disproportionately harm Black individuals.

But here's the thing: we all share one planet. Toxins that seep into the land and fill the sky cannot be contained cleanly within the "sacrifice zone." Hurricanes devastate both wealthy and impoverished populations. There is no such thing as a zero-sum game when it comes to climate change. There is loss everywhere. And interracial organizing is the only way to oppose it. Initiatives such as the Green New Deal represent strong coalitions of activists of all races who are unified in their opposition to the fossil fuel business. Native American leaders led the Standing Rock protests, which were supported by a large number of people. These campaigns have been so effective because they recognized the role of racial hatred in climate change and took aggressive actions to combat it.

CHAPTER SEVEN

Segregation is detrimental to all communities.

When you think about racial segregation, you generally think of low-income areas full of people of color who are ignored by the government and cannot access good schools or social services.

The mostly white suburbs, with their spacious houses and immaculate gardens, may appear to be unaffected by the impacts of segregation. And it is true that white communities are free of the police oppression and neglect that plagues Black communities. However, there are additional expenses to segregation that they must bear.

The main point here is that segregation harms all communities.

In the United States, segregation is not an accident. It has been meticulously designed over generations. The

Homestead Act of 1862 granted American citizens free land plundered from indigenous populations. Of obviously, black people did not qualify for citizenship. This land's richness continues to benefit almost 46 million white descendants. Through discriminatory housing regulations and redlining, Jim Crow laws that existed from the late nineteenth century further reinforced this segregation.

While it is no longer lawful to openly prohibit Black people from purchasing in white districts, economic segregation is nevertheless enforced through exclusive zoning regulations. These allow communities to prohibit the construction of apartment buildings and to specify the size of dwellings. Given the economic legacy of centuries of discriminatory policies, most Black buyers find white neighborhoods economically expensive. But the consequences don't stop there. These regulations have stifled the creation of affordable homes and raised costs, resulting in a massive housing crisis for all poor and middle-class Americans.

Segregated suburbs inevitably result in segregated public schools. This is not simply hazardous to youngsters of color. Isolation and cultural uniformity affect white children as well. According to studies, white children in integrated schools acquire greater critical thinking and problem-solving skills. Furthermore, kids gain the critical skill of cultural competency. Learning to collaborate with people who look different than you is an important ability in an increasingly diversified society - and planet. However, it is one that increasingly isolated white people are missing out on. In fact, 75% of white people in the United States say their social circle is exclusively white. The potential utility of interconnected neighborhoods is nearly limitless. But, in order to do so, we must actively seek to dismantle a racist geography that has been in place for generations.

CHAPTER EIGHT

To undo centuries of structural racism, we need focused remedies.

When the coronavirus hit the United States with a vengeance in early 2020, Americans referred to the epidemic as "color blind." Indeed, it appeared that no one could escape the virus's clutches, rich or poor, politician or waiter.

However, it quickly became evident that, while the virus was colorblind in terms of who became infected, its victims were not all impacted in the same way. Black and Latinx persons were far more likely to die from the virus, owing to variables such as working in dangerous frontline professions, living in areas with higher levels of air pollution, and lacking medical insurance, among others.

The main point is that we need specific measures to address centuries of institutional racism.

Because of a lengthy legacy of discriminatory, racist practices, people of color have died in disproportionate numbers. In the year 2020, this is the reality of life in the United States. While racism harms everyone, those of color suffer the most.

While inter-racial solidarity is necessary, it does not imply that everyone should be treated equally. White people who claim not to recognize race are actually blind to the effects of systemic racism. The only way to build a healthy, integrated society that works for everyone is to explicitly acknowledge the impacts of racism and fight to repair the damage that has been done.

How are we going to do that? Economic policy should be tailored to reduce racial disparity. Consider the case of home ownership. Due to redlining and other discriminatory tactics, Black people continue to lag far behind white homeowners today. A level playing field would go a long way toward closing the wealth divide. However, this will not be accomplished through "colorblind" mortgage tax incentives that favor the already wealthy.

Instead, programs that directly address inequality are required. Instead of disregarding the 1930s' awful redlining maps, you may use them as a roadmap to teach you which areas to focus on first in terms of offering cheap mortgages and beginning financing.

According to zero-sum reasoning, these initiatives are extremely unfair to white people. But, as we've seen, what helps the most oppressed also helps the rest of us. There are significant economic benefits in addition to the enormous social gains. If the US government openly tackled inequality through programs like this, the economy could grow by up to $8 trillion by 2050 as a result of an expanded and reinvigorated middle class.

CHAPTER NINE

Integration and inter-racial organizing generate massive solidarity dividends.

In the 1990s, the little Maine town of Lewiston was on the verge of becoming a ghost town. The city, which was once a booming industrial centre, was hollowed out as firms shuttered and jobs were shipped overseas. As more people went in pursuit of job elsewhere, a vicious loop formed. Most of the storefronts on Main Street were soon vacant.

This depressing story has a pleasant ending. Lewiston is now a bustling city once more. The industrial employment never returned, but an inflow of immigrants has resulted in new entrepreneurs moving into storefronts, producing new jobs and resulting in the establishment of new schools.

The main point is that integration and cross-racial organizing generate significant solidarity benefits.

Thousands of Somali and other African immigrants now call Lewiston home. If white Lewiston citizens had accepted the zero-sum theory that suggested Black people's gain could only come at their expense, they would have been outraged. Instead, many long-term locals welcomed the immigrants.

The Unity Barbecue has become a gathering point for individuals of various backgrounds. Thousands of people have been mobilized by multiracial activist groups to fight for – and win – a state-wide expansion of Medicare and opioid-crisis measures. Lewiston residents have received a massive solidarity dividend.

This demonstrates that white people will not suffer when black people prosper. Actually, everyone will benefit. The African immigrant, the Black single mother, or the Mexican worker harvesting your tomatoes are not the adversaries of economic advancement. The enemy is a small elite that is working together to deprive everyone - black and white - of their standard of living. These are the unscrupulous bureaucrats who pollute your air, the politicians who decide you don't deserve proper healthcare, and the firms that pay starving wages. The 1%

of the population that is now richer than the whole middle class.

This privileged minority has a vested interest in creating racial animosity and pitting us against one another. It understands that cross-racial solidarity is powerful and thus dangerous. Despite the torrent of racist, anti-immigrant rhetoric from outlets such as Fox News, more and more people are seeing through the lies. Multiracial coalitions are attempting to develop environmental and economic policies that benefit the majority rather than the minority. They want to see a world full of gleaming public pools free to any child who wants to swim on a hot summer day.

LAST CHAPTER

In conclusion

The main point of these blinks is:

Tens of millions of Americans are suffering as a result of economic policies that are meant to drain public resources and route money to the top 1% - a billionaire elite that is wealthier than the whole middle class combined. Despite this, white people continue to back politicians that favor billionaires over them. We can't grasp this irrational behavior unless we understand racial identity politics and how conservative politicians stoke the flames of racism for personal advantage. Americans of all races can work together to change their country into one of opportunity and prosperity by challenging white supremacy.

Made in United States
Troutdale, OR
08/04/2023

11823955R00024